2. Allegory of the study of nature, engraving and etching
by Jan Wandelaar, Dutch, 1690–1759
in *Hortus Cliffortianus* (Amsterdam, 1738)
by Carl Linnaeus, Swedish, 1707–1778

THE ILLUSTRATED GARDEN

BOOKS FROM THE MISSOURI BOTANICAL GARDEN
1485–1855

AN EXHIBITION AT THE SAINT LOUIS ART MUSEUM

Francesca Herndon-Consagra

 MISSOURI BOTANICAL GARDEN

St. Louis, MO

PUBLISHED IN THE UNITED STATES BY:

MISSOURI BOTANICAL GARDEN
P.O. Box 299
St. Louis, MO 63166-0299
www.mobot.org

ISBN 1–930723–31–8

Cataloging-in-Publication Data available upon request.

1 2 3 4 5 04 05 06 07 08

FIG. 1 (frontispiece):
detail of **Tulips**, colored mezzotint
by Richard Earlom, British, 1743–1822
after Philipp Reinagle, English, 1749–1833
in *The Temple of Flora* (London, 1807)
by Robert John Thornton, English, c.1768–1837

Right:
detail of **Satin poppy**
see FIG. 38

AUTHOR'S ACKNOWLEDGMENTS

The exhibition "The Illustrated Garden" and its accompanying catalog are products of a truly
enjoyable and collaborative venture by two important cultural institutions in St. Louis.
We are indebted to the directors, staff, and volunteers of the Saint Louis Art Museum and the
Missouri Botanical Garden Library, who have helped in the compilation of this catalog and
assisted with the organization of the exhibition. At the Garden thanks is especially due to
Douglas Holland, Jonathan Kleinbard, Linda Oestry, George E. Schatz, James Solomon, and
Connie Wolf who offered their enthusiasm, expertise, and advice. We are also grateful to
Victoria McMichael and Mary Stiffler for their kindness and assistance.

Marcia Hart, Betsy Newman, and Mary Ott volunteered many hours in the rare book
room of the Missouri Botanical Garden searching for beautiful illustrations. The following
students from Washington University in St. Louis were especially helpful in the selection
and the research of the Garden's botanical books: Kristyna Comer, Heidi Dolamore,
Joseph Fox, Kimberly Kern, and Rebekah Tipping.

For the catalog, we are grateful for the expertise of Elizabeth McNulty and Justin Visnesky
at the Missouri Botanical Garden, as well as the assistance of Jon Cournoyer, Heidi Dolamore,
and Mary Ann Steiner of the Saint Louis Art Museum. The excellent digital photography was
funded by the Andrew W. Mellon Foundation at the Missouri Botanical Garden and done by
Fred Keusenkothen. For the conservation of the prints and books displayed in the exhibition,
we are grateful to Sheba Haner at the Saint Louis Art Museum and to Deborah Wender
and the staff of the Northeast Document Conservation Center.

Table of Contents

FOREWORD

The founding of the Saint Louis Art Museum and the founding of the Missouri Botanical Garden were separated by a mere twenty years: the Garden opened in 1859 and the St. Louis School and Museum of Fine Arts in 1879. Geographically we are only a few miles apart. Our most important similarity, however, is that we have shared since our beginnings a deep commitment to enhancing the cultural richness of the St. Louis region.

The citizens of St. Louis have long understood and endorsed this commitment: the Art Museum was the first in our nation to be publicly funded and today both the Art Museum and the Garden are among the St. Louis cultural institutions that receive the financial support of the community through the Zoo-Museum District.

This exhibition originated in the unique spirit of collaboration that infuses St. Louis's cultural institutions. In 2001, Dr. Francesca Herndon-Consagra, curator of prints, drawings, and photographs at the Art Museum, asked to see the Garden's seventeenth-century illustrated books by Giovanni Battista Ferrari (FIGS. 15, 16), which she had researched as a graduate student. She discovered that the Garden owned not one, but multiple copies of these rare works. The Garden's splendid collection of botanical illustration is among the best in the nation and is distinguished among rare book collections in that its beautiful and fragile volumes remain in use by botanists from around the world.

The exhibition and catalog are the culmination of the research prepared by the two institutions, led by Dr. Herndon-Consagra, and carried out with the assistance of the staff and research facilities of the Art Museum, the Garden, and Washington University in St. Louis. We are delighted to present these great works for exhibition at the Saint Louis Art Museum, so that the people of our community can see these remarkable illustrations and understand their use, their purpose, their importance, and their great beauty.

We are deeply grateful to the William T. Kemper Foundation–Commerce Bank, Trustee; the Monsanto Fund; and The Spoehrer Charitable Trust for the underwriting that made this exhibition possible. A generous contribution from Margaret B. Grigg has supported the publication of the catalog. All of the donors who support the Garden, the Art Museum, and a wide array of other institutions in our region merit our thanks and gratitude for the cultural richness their thoughtful generosity provides.

The catalog includes an essay by Dr. Herndon-Consagra on botanical illustration and an essay by Douglas Holland, the administrator of the Garden Library, on the history and use of these books at the Garden. We hope you enjoy the exhibition and the catalog, and that you visit the Art Museum and the Garden often. They are St. Louis treasures.

Brent R. Benjamin
Director
Saint Louis Art Museum

Peter H. Raven
Director
Missouri Botanical Garden

3. **Tropical lilac,** hand-colored etching
by Johann Scharf, Austrian, 1765–1794
or Martin Sedelmayer, Austrian, 1776–1799
or Franz Anton von Scheidel, Austrian, 1731–1801
in *Plantarum rariorum horti*
caesarei Schoenbrunnensis, vol.1 (Vienna, 1797)
by Nicolaus Joseph Jacquin, Dutch (active Austria), 1712–1817

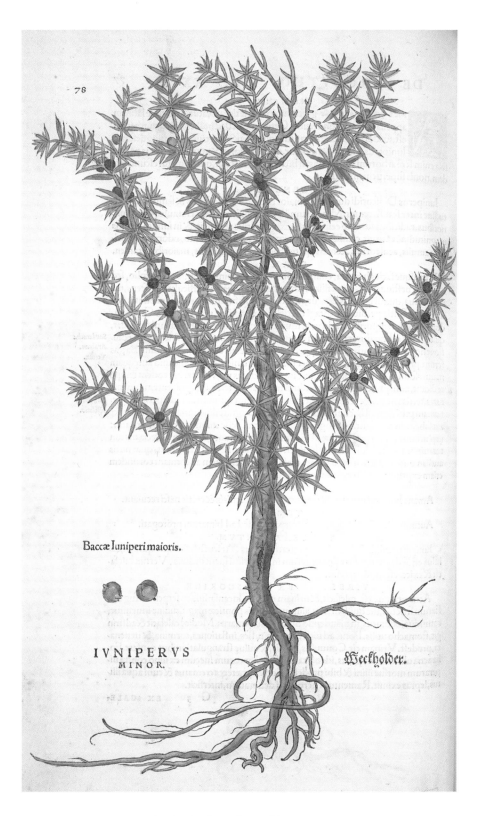

4. **Juniper,** hand-colored woodcut and letterpress
by Veit Rudolf Speckle, German, died before 1550
and Heinrich Füllmaurer, German, c.1500–1547 or 1548
after Albrecht Meyer, German, c.1510–died after 1561
in *De historia stirpium* (Basel, 1542)
by Leonhart Fuchs, German, 1501–1566

INTRODUCTION

by Douglas Holland

The beautiful grounds of the Missouri Botanical Garden established by Henry Shaw in 1859 are quite well known to most residents of St. Louis, but many of its other riches and resources are less familiar. The Missouri Botanical Garden Library is one of these hidden treasures and ranks among the finest botanical libraries in the world.

From its beginnings as a small collection of horticultural books owned by the Garden's founder Henry Shaw, the library has grown to over 170,000 volumes, containing a significant portion the world's accumulated knowledge of plants. Today, the Missouri Botanical Garden Library is well known to the global plant science community as an outstanding research library with a comprehensive collection of rare botanical and horticulture literature, the earliest of which was printed in 1474.

Because of our nature as a research facility, and because of the age and delicacy of many items, access to the collection must be limited. We are therefore especially pleased and privileged to have the opportunity to display these works at the Saint Louis Art Museum, allowing them to be appreciated by a broader audience. The hundred rare works presented in this beautifully curated exhibit are truly precious, not only in their value as fine art and antiques, but as crucial information required by the worldwide botanical research community.

The classification and naming of plants is fundamentally tied to its literature. Unlike some fields of science, botany depends heavily upon publications of the eighteenth and nineteenth centuries to maintain a stable system of names for plants. Under the rules of the International Code of Botanical Nomenclature, any botanist dealing with the names of plants must account for all relevant names published since the formalization of the naming system. Since the genus-species "binomial" system was established with the publication of Carl Linnaeus's *Species Plantarum* in 1753, that means botanists must consult over 250 years of books and journals, often on a daily basis.

Botanical works published before 1753, often called "Pre-Linnaean," can also remain important to modern science. As recently as 2002, Missouri Botanical Garden botanist Dr. Henk van der Werff cited the beautiful illustration of an avocado in Hans Sloane's *A Voyage to the Islands Madera, Barbadoes, Nieves, S. Christophers and Jamaica* (London, 1725) as the representative "type" specimen for that fruit (FIG. 21). In the absence of a historical specimen of dried plant material, botanists can site illustrations, and in some cases might even prefer to do so because of the superior level of detail.

A great deal of credit for assembling this collection of early botanical books is owed to the Garden's first director, Dr. William Trelease. From his first days as director in 1889, Trelease was convinced of the importance of a great library to the Garden and was closely involved in its development. Through the friendship he cultivated with Edward Lewis Sturtevant, the Garden acquired what would become the core of the collection.

A native and lifelong resident of New England, Sturtevant was trained as a physician though he never practiced, preferring instead to focus on agriculture. Widely known for his writings on dairy cattle, Sturtevant also had a fascination with useful and edible plants, culminating in the publication of Sturtevant's *Notes on Edible Plants* in 1919. In support of his interest, he assembled a significant collection of herbals and other early printed books about plants and their uses. In 1892 Sturtevant donated his entire collection to the Missouri Botanical Garden. His gift came with no conditions, only with the "strong desire" that it would continue to "serve a purpose." When the last of seventeen crates had arrived and was unpacked, the Garden's new collection numbered over 500 books, representing one of the greatest Pre-Linnaean botanical libraries ever assembled.

Trelease continued to build the collection with another significant purchase in 1902 from the European bookseller, W.W. Junk. This collection of more than 600 volumes supplemented the gaps in the Sturtevant collection and with it, Trelease completed the important foundation for the future of the library. Over the next one hundred years the collection continued to grow through donations and careful purchases and today holds over 1,000 books printed before 1753 and over 10,000 books printed before 1850.

Some rare book collections operate with a sole goal of preservation. The collection at the Missouri Botanical Garden Library exists both to preserve and use. It is a working collection with a mission of providing botanical information to our own research staff as well as a global research community. As stewards of this collection, our challenge is to meet the sometimes conflicting goals of access and preservation.

Since 1997 the library has been stored in state-of-the-art facilities with rigorous security, temperature, and humidity controls as well as protection from earthquakes. However, the demands of usage still produce wear and tear. New technologies can allow greater access to the collection, while reducing damage. For example, several of the books in this exhibit have been digitized and made available on the Internet. Though electronic facsimile does not replace the tactile experience of the original, availability of the digital books minimize handling of the original while making these rare publications available to millions of readers.

The Missouri Botanical Garden Library continues to fulfill our mission by collecting botanical literature of all time periods and languages. Our collection ranges from the early books presented here to the most recently published literature, increasingly in electronic format, and in dozens of languages. These materials are available to researchers around the world via our online library catalog and interlibrary loan.

We hope you enjoy this catalog and exhibit and continue to study and marvel at the beauty of early botanical books and the magnificent collection of those books available at the Missouri Botanical Garden Library.

MAGNOLIA Lauri folio subtus albicante, Catesb. T.I. p. 39. Dill.
H. Elth. p. 207. Mill. Gard. dict.

5. **Sweet bay magnolia,** hand-colored etching and engraving
by Johann Jakob Haid, German, 1704–1767
after Georg Dionysius Ehret, German, 1708–1770
in *Plantae selectae*, part 1 (Nuremberg, 1750)
by Cristoph Jacob Trew, German, 1695–1769

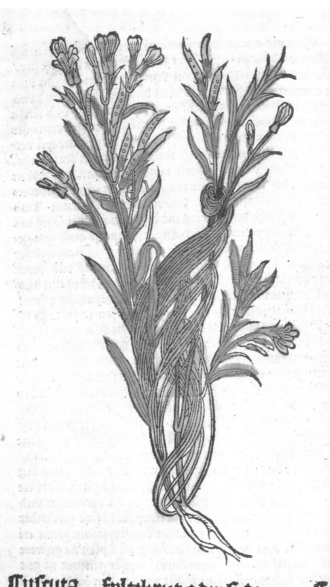

Cuſcuta   fyltzkrut oder ſyde   Cap·xcij·

Dſcuta latine·grece hadorafa·arabice Laſuch·   Serapio
in dem büch aggregatoris in dē capitel Laſuch id eſt Cuſcu
ta ſpricht daz diß krut kncket ſich vmb die baiim vnd iſt ge/
ſtalt glich als garn an dem ſtengel·vñ an der ſpitzen hait eß eyn ſub
tyel frucht·Man fyndet eß vil in dem flaße·Syn natuer iſt heyß an
dem erſten grade vñ drucken an dem andern·   Auch ſtat geſchriebē

6, 7. **Dodder** (above); **Dodder and chickory** (right); woodcuts with
watercolor applied via stencil and freehand and letterpress
by an unknown artist
in *Gart der Gesundheyt* (Mainz, 1485)
published by Peter Schöffer, German, c. 1425–c.1502

THE ILLUSTRATED GARDEN

The Missouri Botanical Garden's extensive collection of rare books has holdings that date back to the fifteenth century. These books are still in use today, aiding botanists as they name and describe flora culled from around the world. Many of the books contain marginalia that reveal the insights of generations of botanists investigating plant classification (FIGS. 9, 10, 36). Botanists approach the works with a scientific eye, analyzing the textual and visual descriptors of a plant. Art enthusiasts, however, gauge the value of a botanical illustration with different considerations in mind: the artistic precision demonstrated in rendering complex shapes and textures, how well the printer inked and printed the sheet, the colorist's skill in applying paint to the print, how sensitively the editor placed the illustration in the layout of the book, and the condition of the paper itself. This essay focuses on the artistic importance of the finest illustrations in the Garden's Library and discusses some of the printing processes used to create them. It regards the books as beautiful examples of the vibrant intellectual and cultural circles of western Europe from 1485 to 1855. Four years later, in 1859, Henry Shaw opened the Missouri Botanical Garden as a center for research.

The oldest illustrated books in the Garden's collection are herbals. Written primarily by physicians, herbals are books about plants and herbs that served as manuals for apothecaries in the preparation of remedies. Printed herbals first appeared in western Europe during the last quarter of the fifteenth century, just after the invention of the printing press, movable type, and the use of woodcuts to illustrate books. *Gart der Gesundheyt* (Garden of Health)—printed in 1485 in Mainz by Peter Schöffer, the inheritor of Gutenberg's printing establishment—is the earliest illustrated book at the Garden. Like most Renaissance herbals, *Gart der Gesundheyt* was based on the writings of the ancients, including such natural scientists as Dioscorides and Pliny the Elder, both of whom compiled descriptions of medicinal plants of the Mediterranean during the first century A.D. Medieval scribes copied such ancient texts and images onto animal skins and papyrus. These copies were often damaged and filled with errors in

8. **Barnacle goose tree,** woodcut and letterpress
   by an unknown artist
   in *The Herball* (London, 1636)
   by John Gerard, English, 1545–1612
   and Thomas Johnson, English, c.1600–1644

transcription. The prevalence of medieval lore sometimes led to the inclusion of fantastic creatures such as geese that hatched from barnacles growing on trees, seen in John Gerard's *Herball* (London, 1636; FIG. 8).

Stylistic variations in the plates of *Gart der Gesundheyt* suggest numerous hands worked on the woodcuts. The shading and depth employed in the drawing of a dodder plant evoke a sense of realism, while other illustrations retain a two-dimensional quality common among medieval herbals (FIGS. 6, 7). Such stylized flatness is evident in the Venetian herbal *Hortus sanitatis* published in 1511 (FIG. 9). Its woodcuts were copied from illustrations in earlier publications and dropped into double column page settings with scant regard for harmony between text and image.

9. **Double page with unidentified plants,** woodcuts and letterpress
   by an unknown artist
   in *Hortus sanitatis* (Venice, 1511)
   edited by Bernardino Benalio, Italian, born c.1458–died after 1543
   and Giovanni Tacuino, Italian, active 1502–1536

European standards for the illustrated herbal improved with the publication of Otto Brunfels's *Herbarium vivae eicones* in 1530 (FIG. 10). Rather than copy illustrations of plants known only in antiquity, artists began to prepare drawings based on direct observation of plants closer to home. Here, three violets are delicately balanced, one on top of the other, to produce a visually appealing calligraphic line that sweeps from one grouping to the other. Brunfels's artist, Hans Weiditz, chose to draw three different examples of the same type of violet rather than create an idealized composite. Weiditz's careful examination led him to depict each specimen with all its faults, appearing as though it had just been pulled from the ground and brought into the studio. In Leonhard Fuchs's *De historia stirpium* (Basel, 1542), the methods of illustration resemble those still preferred today. His artists combined observation of nature with stylization, utilizing multiple specimens to create an exemplar, rather than make an exact reproduction of a particular specimen (FIGS. 4, 11).

By the mid-sixteenth century, European expeditions to foreign lands generated a flood of new information as explorers documented and collected specimens while abroad. Imports like vanilla, coffee, tea, and cocoa proved immensely lucrative, momentous to colonial land use, and revolutionary to European cuisine and medicine. These discoveries not only spurred the desire to produce illustrated botanical books, they also fostered patronage of further plant research. As early as the 1540s, universities and wealthy collectors throughout Europe funded professorships and botanical gardens, and they established collections of dried plants known as herbaria. These vast arrays of plants included varieties not native to the region, providing a unique point of reference for detailed study. The number of described species kept pace with increased efforts at research, jumping from approximately 500 recorded in 1485 to 7,700 in the 1750s; today estimates are as high as 420,000.

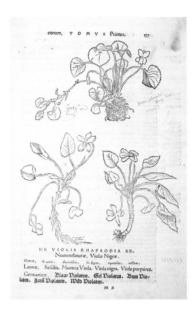

10. **Violets,** woodcut and letterpress
by Hans Weiditz, German,
born before 1500–c.1536
in *Herbarum vivae eicones* (Strasbourg, 1530)
by Otto Brunfels, German, 1488–1534

11. **Artists of *De historia stirpium*,** woodcut and letterpress
by Veit Rudolf Speckle, German, died 1590
and Heinrich Füllmaurer, German, c.1500–1547 or 1548
after Albrecht Meyer, German, c.1510–died after 1561
in *De historia stirpium* (Basel, 1542)
by Leonhart Fuchs, German, 1501–1566

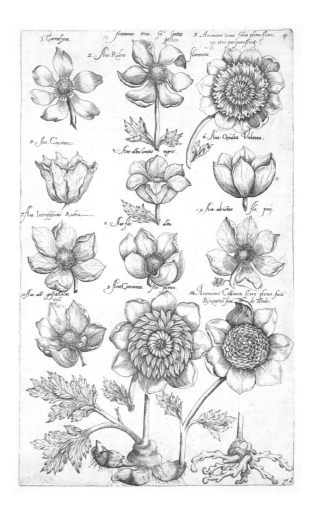

I 2. **Anemones**, engraving
by an unknown artist
in *Florilegium* (Amsterdam, 1647–1654)
by Emanuel Sweerts, Dutch, 1552–1612

An unparalleled passion for exotic flowers developed as a direct consequence of foreign trade, and it called for a new kind of book, the *florilegium*. Intended for collectors, these books celebrated flowers for their aesthetic qualities. First published in Amsterdam in 1612, the *Florilegium* of Emanuel Sweerts, a Dutch floriculturist and plant dealer, provided a type of catalog for selling plants and bulbs (FIG. 12). Plants took hold of the imaginations and purse strings of the *virtuosi*, or the university-educated dilettantes of the aristocracy and the wealthy merchant classes. They sought to own gardens filled with the latest exotics—tulips, irises, amaryllises, anemones, and citrus—many of which were extremely expensive and difficult to cultivate. Johann Christoph Volkamer's *Hesperides* (Nuremberg, 1713) provides a glimpse into the private gardens of Germany around 1700, with their fanciful parterres, potted citrus fruits, and fountains (FIG. 13). Patrician flower collectors funded important publications to publicize their botanical collections and enhance their status in society. More importantly, they patronized scholars, botanists, scientists, and horticulturalists, who were then able to produce lavish publications that advanced the study of botany.

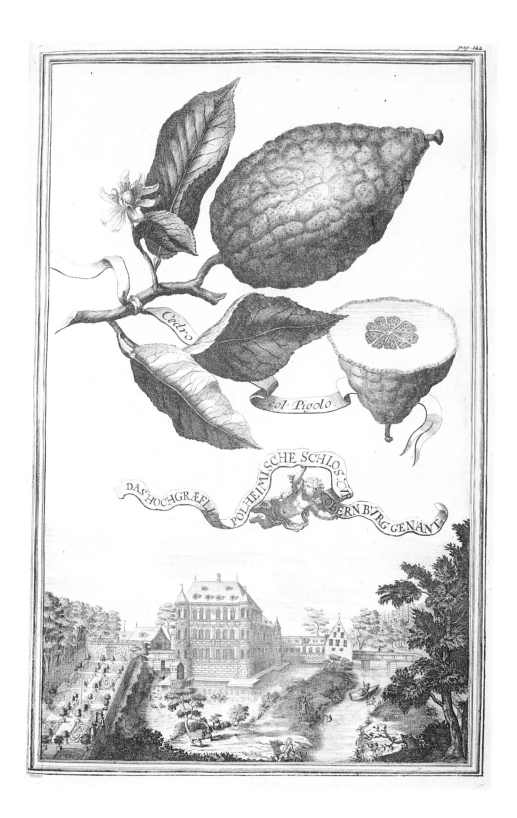

13. **Citron with view of a castle in Obernburg**, etching and engraving
by an unknown artist
in *Hesperides norimbergenses* (Nuremberg, 1713)
by Johann Christoph Volkamer, German, 1644–1720

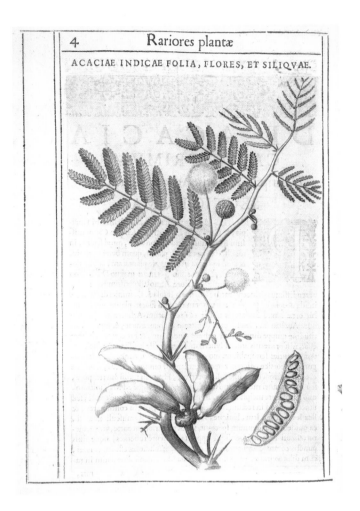

14. **Sweet acacia**, engraving
   attributed to Luca Ciamberlano, Italian, 1586–1641
   after drawings attributed to Pietro Castelli, Italian, c.1575–c.1657
   in *Exactissima descriptio rariorum quarundam plantarum* (Rome, 1625)
   by Tobia Aldini, Italian, dates unknown
   and Pietro Castelli

Rome became one of the most important centers of scientific activity in the first half of the seventeenth century, producing remarkable botanical books devoted to rare plants. Scientific societies like the Accademia dei Lincei and the patronage of papal families encouraged the natural sciences to flourish. Learned botanists such as Johann Faber of Bamberg held professorships at the University of Rome while nearby, Galileo Galilei investigated the universe. In 1625 Cardinal Odoardo Farnese sponsored a publication devoted to the exotics in his family's splendid gardens. Closely tied to the Jesuit order, the Farnese collected rare seeds and plants harvested by missionary priests in India, China, and the West Indies. Many of these plants were published for the first time in Tobia Aldini and Pietro Castelli's *Exactissima descriptio...plantarum* (Rome, 1625; FIG. 14). Giovanni Battista Ferrari's *Flora* and *Hesperides*

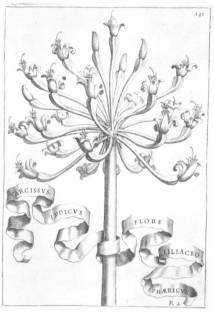

15. Chandelier lily, engraving
   after Nicolas de la Fleur, French, c.1600–1663
   in *Flora overo cultura di fiori* (Rome, 1638)
   by Giovanni Battista Ferrari, Italian, 1584–1655

16. Citrus, engraving
   by Cornelis Bloemart, Dutch, 1603–c.1684
   after Vincenzo Leonardi, Italian, active 1621–1646
   or Domenico Bonavena, Italian, dates unknown
   in *Hesperides* (Rome, 1646)
   by Giovanni Battista Ferrari, Italian, 1584–1655

(Rome, 1638; Rome, 1646) reflect the intellectual achievements of influential artists and scholars in the service of Cardinal Francesco Barberini, whose collection of exotics equaled, if not surpassed, that of the Farnese (FIGS. 15, 16). This passion for rare plants diminished the dependence on dried specimens from abroad because artists were able to execute their splendid images after observing such exotics actually blooming in these important collections.

The rudimentary microscopes that were invented around 1600 surfaced in scientific circles throughout Europe in the following decades. By the mid-1630s, close examination of plant anatomy started to replace superficial observation, with microscopes opening the way to observing finer details of nature. In 1635 Ferrari mentions using a microscope to analyze a hibiscus seed illustrated in his *Flora*. Robert Hooke's invention of the compound microscope, the first to resemble microscopes in use today, allowed him to produce some of the finest microscopic engravings ever made. His *Micrographia* of 1665 was the first book devoted to microscopic observations, and included his examination of such common things as fish scales, fleas, and human hair along with cork and sponges, many of which were drawn and engraved by the author himself. Hooke discovered the cellular structure of cork, shown here, which

17. **Cell construction of cork with an acacia branch**, etching attributed to Robert Hooke, English, 1605–1703 in *Micrographia* (London, 1665) by Robert Hooke

helped open a whole new world of plant anatomy (FIG. 17). Aided in his research by microscopes, Marcello Malphighi published the first book on plant anatomy in 1675. Nehemiah Grew's investigations included the identification of stamens and pistils as male and female sex organs in his groundbreaking book *The Anatomy of Plants* (London, 1682), which features wonderfully detailed etchings of cross sections of dandelions (FIG. 18). However, it was not until Rudolf Jacob Camerarius's letter on the sexes of plants in 1694 that the mechanism of plant fertilization was fully understood. Research into plant anatomy revealed the utter inaccuracy of some of the more imaginative plants like the "Man-carrying orchid," illustrated in the first medical journal (Leipzig, 1671; FIG. 19). Before the understanding of plant sexual systems in the 1690s, it was not inconceivable to imagine small men blooming from orchids!

18. detail of **Cross-section of dandelion stem**, etching by an unknown artist in *The Anatomy of Plants* (London, 1682) by Nehemiah Grew, English, 1641–1712

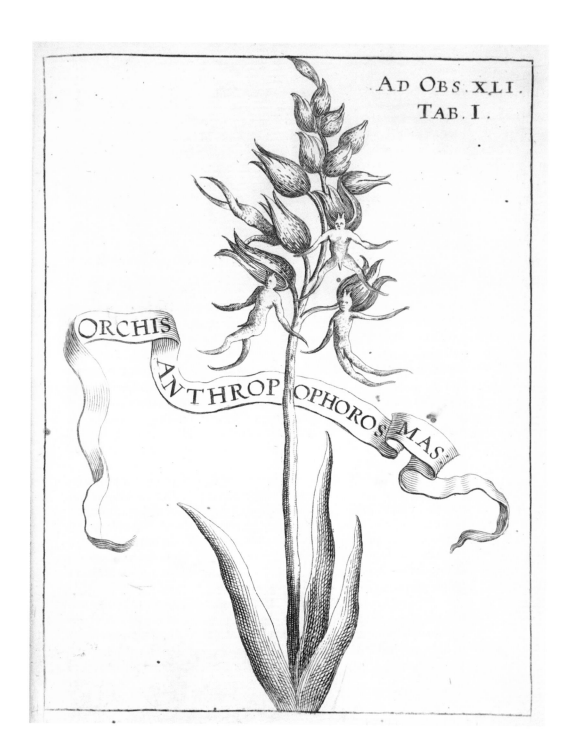

19. "Man-carrying orchid," engraving and etching
by an unknown artist
in *Miscellanea curiosa medico-physica*, vol. 2 (Leipzig, 1671)
published by Academia Naturae Curiosorum

20, 21. Air plant and Spanish moss with other flora (right),
Lignum vitae, Jamaican plum, and avocado (below), engraving and etchings
by Michael Vandergucht, Flemish (active England), 1660–1725
and John Savage, English, active 1680–1700
after Everhardus Kickius, nationality and dates unknown
in *A Voyage to the Islands Madera, Barbadoes, Nieves,
S. Christophers and Jamaica* (London, 1707–1725)
by Sir Hans Sloane, English, 1660–1753

A better understanding of plant morphology, combined with pictorial imagination and technical skill, aided plant illustrators in bringing dried specimens to life on the printed page. Sir Hans Sloane, an English physician whose collection became the cornerstone of the British Museum's holdings, worked in Jamaica from 1687 to 1689. Sloane collected 800 species of plants, some of which were new to Europe. His contribution to the demand for foreign goods, including seeds and plants, had agricultural and economic implications. Sloane spent most of his free time collecting samples of Caribbean flora and fauna that he later published in his natural history (FIGS. 20, 21). For that volume, a local Anglican minister drew the flora that Sloane could not send home, while his artists in England relied primarily upon dried specimens shipped from Jamaica, skillfully infusing dimension and grace into their illustrations and crafting them to resemble live specimens.

22. Cane toad, lizard, and stylized vine, etching
by an unknown artist
in *Locupletissimi rerum naturalium thesauri*
(Amsterdam, 1734–1765)
by Albert Seba, Dutch, 1665–1736

The artists hired by Albert Seba made no such attempt to recreate live plants when they were representing Seba's natural history collection. Instead, their flat arrangements of dried plants resemble decorative friezes: in one plate, a stylized vine symmetrically frames a toad and a lizard (FIG. 22). Seba, a Dutch apothecary, commissioned a pictorial record of his extensive private collection which he gathered from the far corners of the earth.

ALBERTVS SEBA, ETZELA OOSTFRISIVS
Pharmacopoeus Amftelaedamenfis
ACAD: CAESAR: LEOPOLDINO CAROLINAE NAT: CVRIOS: COLLEGA XENOCRATES DICTVS;
SOCIET: REG: ANGLICANAE, et ACAD: SCIENTIAR: BONONIENSIS INSTITVTVS SODALIS.
AETATIS LXVI. ANNO CDDCCXXXI.

23, 24. Albert Seba with his natural history cabinet (above), etching
by Jacob Houbraken, Dutch, 1698–1780
Nine-banded armadillo with yellow wood, crossberry,
ice plant, and other flora (right), etching
by an unknown artist
in *Locupletissimi rerum naturalium thesauri* (Amsterdam, 1734–1765)
by Albert Seba, Dutch, 1665–1736

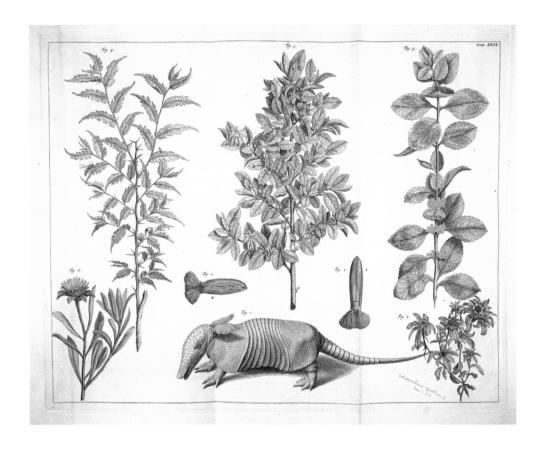

In the frontispiece of the book, Jacob Houbraken depicts Seba seated in his cabinet of curiosities, surrounded by shelves full of jarred specimens, sketches depicting plants and animals, and his renowned collection of seashells (FIG. 23). Seba obtained many of his curios from sailors; when a ship arrived in port, Seba hastened to the harbor and made purchases or bartered his medications. The book presents attractive compositions of dried specimens and disregards habitat when selecting species to accompany one another on a single plate. An American armadillo, for instance, appears next to a group of plants considered Ethiopian at the time (FIG. 24).

The English naturalist Mark Catesby sought instead to portray the organic relationships between flora and fauna in his great work, *The Natural History of Carolina, Florida, and the Bahama Islands* (London, 1754). Although Catesby lacked formal artistic training, he prepared drawings to accompany his descriptions, and when he was unable to secure the funds for an etcher, Catesby undertook the project himself, etching the copperplates and coloring the finished pages during the early stages of production. He writes: "In designing the Plants, I always did them while fresh and just gathered: and the Animals, particularly the Bird, I painted while alive (except a very few)… I have adapted the Birds to those Plants on which they fed, or have any relation to." Catesby depicts a tyrant flycatcher catching an insect while perched on its favorite nesting tree, the sassafras (FIG. 25). His emphasis on patient and careful observations in the field strongly influenced later depictions of American natural history, notably John James Audubon's *Birds of America* (London, 1827–1838).

As artists became more knowledgeable about plants, their illustrations became more detailed and intricate. These prints, in turn, became especially helpful to botanists in establishing a system of classification. During the first half of the eighteenth century, the Swedish botanist Carl Linnaeus combed through botanical literature, correlating the observations and descriptions of other naturalists. Linnaeus used illustrations to establish exemplars for numerous species. In 1735 Linnaeus introduced a system of classifying plants by genus and species—a binomial nomenclature that survived the upheavals of Darwinian evolution and remains in use today. Thus, all roses are grouped in the genus *Rosa*, and all oaks in the genus *Quercus*. Each genus, or group, is comprised of one or more species made up of closely related organisms with shared structural attributes. For example, *Quercus* contains the pin oak (*Quercus palustris*) and the black oak (*Quercus velutina*) along with many other species, whereas the genus *Ginkgo* consists of only a single species. Latin binomials became the standard after the publication of Linnaeus's *Species Plantarum* in 1753. Linnaeus also proposed a simple method for classifying plants based upon the number stamens and pistils. This artificial system provided a practical approach for sorting and identifying that even an amateur botanist or gardener could employ.

25. **Sassafras and tyrant flycatcher,** hand-colored etching
by Mark Catesby, English, c.1682–1749
in *The Natural History of Carolina, Florida,
and the Bahama Islands,* vol. 1 (London, 1754)
by Mark Catesby

Cornus mas Odorata.
Safsafras.

Muscicapa Corona rubra.
The Tyrant.

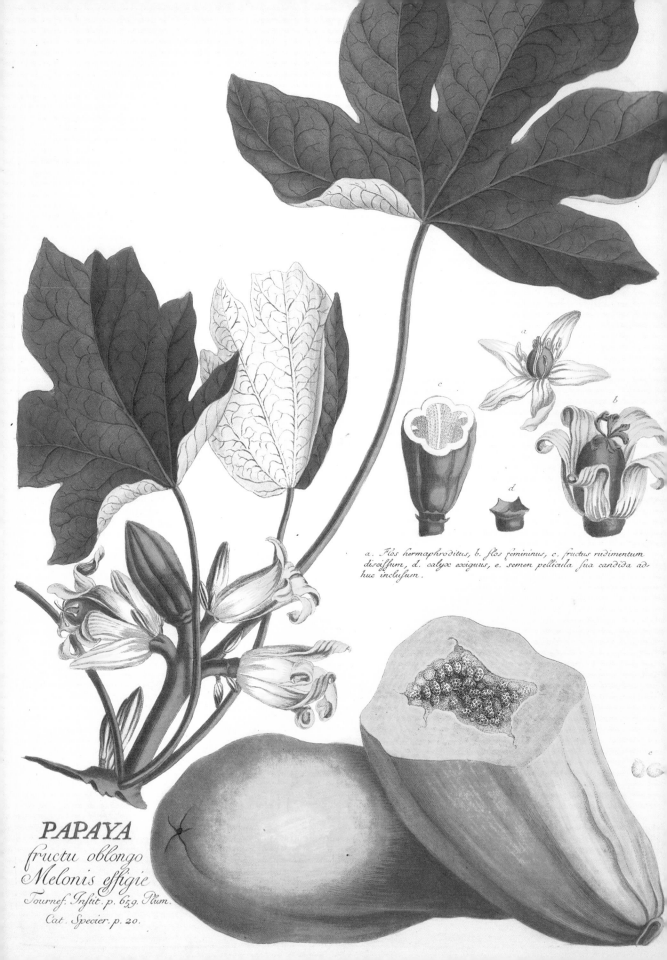

a. *Flos hermaphroditus,* b. *flos femininus,* c. *fructus rudimentum discissum,* d. *calyx exiguus,* e. *semen pellicula sua candida adhuc inclusum.*

PAPAYA
fructu oblongo
Melonis effigie
Tournef. Instit. p. 659. Plum.
Cat. Specier. p. 20.

Linnaeus's scientific work profoundly affected the illustrations of Georg Dionysius Ehret, who in turn influenced generations of botanical illustrators. Ehret worked directly with Linnaeus on the *Hortus Cliffortianus* (Amsterdam, 1738; Fig. 2) that described the collection of plants owned by George Clifford, a banker and director of the Dutch East India Company with an extraordinary private estate called Hartekamp near Haarlem, Holland. Clifford was fascinated by Linnaeus's ability to classify plants that were unknown to him simply by looking at the parts of the flower. For the illustrations to the *Hortus Cliffortianus*, Linnaeus instructed Ehret to analyze the structure of a plant before attempting to depict it. The botanist remarked on Ehret's development over the course of their collaboration: "Ehret did in the beginning absolutely not want to paint the stamina, pisitilla, and other small parts, as he argued they would spoil the drawing; in the end he gave in, however, and then he liked this kind of work so much that thereafter he observed the most minute...particulars." Ehret created beautifully composed images of blossoms next to detailed cross sections of the sexual parts in his work for *Plantae selectae* (Nuremberg, 1750–1773; Figs. 5, 26).

26. **Papaya**, hand-colored etching and engraving
by Johann Jakob Haid, German, 1704–1767
after Georg Dionysius Ehret, German, 1708–1770
in *Plantae selectae,* part 1 (Nuremberg, 1750)
by Cristoph Jacob Trew, German, 1695–1769

The Linnaean emphasis on the blossom produced illustrative work so beautifully detailed that it is reminiscent of Baroque flower painting. One of the greatest floral artists of all time, Pierre Joseph Redouté is heir to the tradition of Dutch flower painting as well as to Ehret's aesthetic principals. The Missouri Botanical Garden owns Redouté's luxurious edition of nearly 500 plates, *Les Liliacées*, published and edited by Redouté himself in eight folio volumes (Paris, 1802–1816). Redouté benefited from the patronage of three successive French queens, and dedicated the chandelier lily depicted in *Les Liliacées* to Empress Joséphine Bonaparte (FIG. 27).

27. **Chandelier lily**, stipple etching with roulette, line engraving, and *à-la-poupée* color printing by Lemaire, French, active 18th century after Pierre Joseph Redouté, French, 1759–1840 in *Les Liliacées*, vol. 7 (Paris, 1813) by François de Laroche, French, 1743–1812

Amaryllis de Josephine.

Lemaire sculp.

Pinus Cembra

28. **Siberian stone pine,** hand-colored stipple and line engraving with roulette
by Warner, English, dates unknown
after Ferdinand Bauer, Austrian, 1760–1826
in *A Description of the Genus Pinus,* vol. 1 (London, 1803)
by Aylmer Bourke Lambert, English, 1761–1842

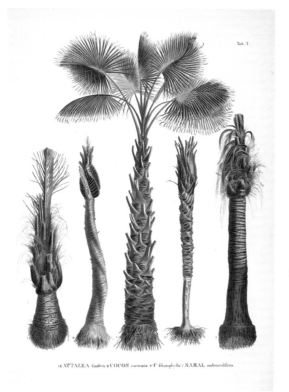

Tab. T.

ıı ATTALEA funifera ıı COCOS coronata ıv C. Schizophylla v SABAL umbraculifera.

29. New world palm trees, hand-colored lithograph
after a drawing attributed to Ferdinand Bauer,
Austrian, 1760–1826
in *Historia naturalis palmarum,*
vol. 1, part 6 (Leipzig, 1837)
by Karl Friedrich Philipp von Martius,
German, 1756–1847

Redouté designed *Les Liliacées* for the wealthy botanical amateur who would admire the beauty of the plants as well as the immense charm of the compositions and the mastery of its color printing. Aylmer Bourke Lambert, on the other hand, created a sumptuous publication intended primarily for botanists. Each copy of *A Description of the Genus Pinus* (London, 1823–1853) is unique, owing to variations in printing and compilation (FIG. 28). Bauer surpassed even Redouté in the accuracy of his illustrations, earning accolades from the German writer and theorist Johann Wolfgang von Goethe for his illustrations in Lambert's book on pines: "Nature is visible, Art concealed."

Linnaeus's artificial system of classification came under attack almost as soon as it was published. Antoine Laurent de Jussieu argued for a natural system in his groundbreaking book, *Genera plantarum* (Paris, 1789), in which he advocated for the organization of plants into families based on morphological characteristics of the entire plant. Followers of Jussieu instructed their artists to include the whole plant since it might not be evident which characteristics would ultimately determine classification. In keeping with this approach, the splendid lithographs of Karl Friedrich Philipp von Martius's *Historia naturalis palmarum* present every aspect of the palm tree (Leipzig, 1823–1850; FIG. 29).

VIGNE

In the nineteenth century the love of gardening and flowers began to traverse social and economic barriers, which greatly contributed to the popularization of floral motifs in the decorative and industrial arts. An increasing number of novices took interest in botany, generating a new readership for some very unconventional flower books. J. J. Grandville's *Les Fleurs animées* (Paris, 1846–1847) addressed an audience of female amateur gardeners and included illustrations of anthropomorphic flowers occupying landscapes that parodied the nature of the flower, its name, or its historical associations (FIGS. 30, 31). Robert Thornton's fantastic *The Temple of Flora* (London, 1807) glorified twenty-six species with lengthy poems and extravagant prose alongside colored illustrations depicting flowers as gigantic entities in fictional landscapes (FIG. 1).

30, 31. **Grapevine** (above),
Daffodil (right), hand-colored etching and engraving
by Charles Geoffroy, French, 1819–1882
after Jean Jacques Grandville, French, 1803–1847
in *Les Fleurs animées* (Paris, 1846–1847)
by Jean Jacques Grandville
and Taxile Delord, French, 1815–1877

Grandville del.   Ch. Geoffroy sc.

NARCISSE

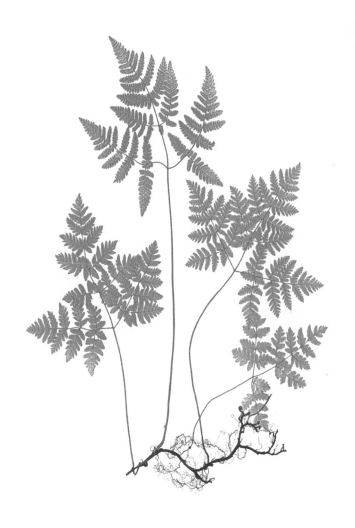

32. Oak fern, nature print
by Henry Bradbury, English, 1829–1860
in *The Ferns of Great Britain
and Ireland* (London, 1855)
by Thomas Moore, English, 1821–1887

As the public enjoyment of botanical literature grew, so did the desire to publish comprehensive catalogs of national floras and to fill gardens with native plants. In the introduction to Thomas Moore's *The Ferns of Great Britain and Ireland*, (London, 1855), the author explains his endeavor: "The present work has been prepared, with the view of showing… what differences really exist among the Ferns which grow wild in Great Britain and Ireland. These beautiful plants of late years attracted so much attention, and are now so universally cultivated, that it has become most desirable to establish on solid grounds the true value of their characteristic marks." (FIGS. 32, 42).

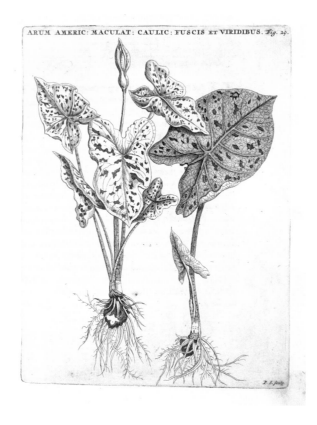

ARUM AMERIC: MACULAT: CAULIC: FUSCIS ET VIRIDIBUS. *Fig. 29.*

33. **Caladium**, etching
    by Pieter Sluiter, Dutch, 1675–died after 1713
    in *Horti medici amstelædamensis* (Leiden, 1706)
    by Caspar Commelin, Dutch, 1668–1731

Through classification, nations claimed plants as regional or indigenous, fostering a national identity separate from that of neighboring states. Before Linnaeus, botanists used a string of descriptive Latin, Greek, and vernacular terms to identify plants, as can be seen in the plant names accompanying the illustrations of Brunfels's violets and Caspar Commelin's caladium (FIGS. 10, 33). Linnaeus's binomial system facilitated the universal naming of plants; these efforts at naming, in turn, established a sense of ownership. Lavishly illustrated, multivolume books of the eighteenth and nineteenth centuries depicting national floras reinforced the state's identity and were an expression of the age of nationalism in western Europe. The *Flora Danica* was among the most ambitious of these projects, endeavoring to depict all plants native to Denmark and Norway (Copenhagen, 1761–1874; FIG. 34).

Traveling through England in 1851, the wealthy Missouri merchant Henry Shaw visited the Royal Botanic Gardens at Kew, the Crystal Palace Exhibition, and Chatsworth—the Duke of Devonshire's estate in Derbyshire. These experiences inspired him to establish a botanical garden in St. Louis. Upon returning to the United States, Shaw began to plan the garden in earnest and planted thousands of trees and shrubs near his country villa on the outskirts of the city. Before opening his garden to the public in 1859, Shaw had the wherewithal to seek advice from a local physician-botanist, Dr. George Englemann, as well as the leading botanists of the day, Asa Gray of Harvard and William Jackson Hooker, director of the Kew Gardens. Hooker wrote to Shaw: "Very few appendages to a garden are of more importance for instruction...than a library and economic museum." In essence, he defined the current focus of the Garden: research, display, and education. Part of this mission included collecting these extraordinary illustrated books. In doing so, Shaw and his successors brought an illustrated garden to the major trading city on the Mississippi with the western frontier at its doorstep. ᴒ❧

34. detail of **Thistle ball**, hand-colored engraving
    by Johann Theodor Bayer, Danish, 1782–1873
    in *Flora Danica*, vol. 13, issue 37 (Copenhagen, 1836)
    edited by Jens Wilken Hornemann, Danish, 1770–1841

PROCESSES

35. **Woodblock of peas,** pearwood
after Giorgio Liberale, Italian, active 16th century
and Wolfgang Meyerpeck, German, active c.1570
for *Commentarii* (Prague, 1562)
by Pietro Andrea Mattioli, Italian, 1500–1577

Botanical books prior to 1600 were primarily illustrated by means of woodblocks that were usually about an inch thick, cut from fine-grained trees such as pear and apple. To make a woodcut, an artist draws directly on the woodblock. A woodcutter uses a knife to cut away wood from the sides of lines that the artist had drawn. When completely cut, the image appears as a network of raised lines, not unlike a modern rubber stamp. The surface of the block is inked and printed on the same press used for movable type. The Garden owns a fine example of a sixteenth-century woodblock depicting peas for Pietro Andrea Mattioli's *Commentarii* (Prague, 1562; FIG. 35).

After 1600 botanical publishers favored the process of intaglio, which includes etchings and engravings. Intaglio prints require a different press than letterpress type. Despite their costliness and the difficulty entailed in integrating image with text, publishers chose these processes because they provided greater detail and clarity than even the best woodcuts. Engraving is a highly skilled art form and requires much practice and time to complete a design. Using a tool called a burin, engravers carve deep, even lines into the surface of a copperplate. Whether straight or curved, engraved lines are typically parallel, resulting in a characteristic clarity that is especially evident in the illustration of the acacia plant in Tobia

Aldini and Pietro Castelli's *Exactissima descriptio...plantarum* (Rome, 1625; FIG. 14). To print an engraving, ink is forced down into the incised lines of the plate, the excess ink is wiped from the surface with a rag, and a sheet of paper is placed on top of the plate. Finally, it is passed through a rolling press.

Etchings, too, are printed from copperplates. Yet etched lines are not carved by hand into the plate. To make an etching, a plate is first coated with a wax or resin ground that is resistant to acid. The artist uses a pointed tool to draw a design into the ground, revealing portions of the copperplate below. Afterward, the plate is immersed in an acid bath that erodes the exposed surface of the plate, producing lines that are "bitten" into the copper. When the ground is removed, the incised lines are ready to receive ink, much like the incised lines of an engraving. This process requires less time to produce an illustration, and is thus much more affordable than an engraving. Pliable etching grounds allow artists to draw freely on the plate; as a result, etchings appear less rigid than engravings. Paul de Reneaulme's *Specimen historiae plantarum* (Paris, 1611) exemplifies the potential of the medium, depicting a cauliflower in such rich detail that it looks as if the actual plant had been pressed on the prepared plate itself (FIG. 36).

36. **Kale and cauliflower,** etching
by an unknown artist
in *Specimen historiae plantarum* (Paris, 1611)
by Paul de Reneaulme, French, 1560–1624

Many of the great publications in the Garden's collection are hand-colored lithographs. Invented in the late 1790s, lithography involves a drawing that is made with a greasy crayon on a slab of limestone. A chemical process transforms the porous stone, causing the greasy areas to repel water, while the remaining surface resists ink. The stone is dampened with water, and a viscous printing ink is applied, which adheres only to the area of the original drawing. Paper is placed on the stone, and the image is transferred from stone to sheet under the pressure of a lithographic press. Not only is this method cheaper and quicker than the intaglio processes, it also enables an adept artist to subtly craft an image on the stone exactly as it would appear, mirrored, on the printed page.

Artists like Walter Hood Fitch drew directly onto the lithographic stone. His accurate and lively renditions of the watercolor drawings by Sir Joseph Dalton Hooker in *Illustrations of Himalayan Plants* (London, 1855) stand as some of the best botanical illustrations of the mid-nineteenth century (FIGS. 37, 38).

Plate IX

MECONOPSIS NEPALENSIS, Wall.

37, 38. detail of **Blue poppy** (left); **Satin poppy** (above), hand-colored lithographs
by Walter Hood Fitch, Scottish, 1817–1892
after Sir Joseph Dalton Hooker, English, 1817–1911
in *Illustrations of Himalayan Plants* (London, 1855)
by Sir Joseph Dalton Hooker

Pl. 24

ODONTOGLOSSOM GRANDE.

The largest botanical book ever produced is James Bateman's *The Orchidaceae of Mexico and Guatemala* (London, 1837–1843) which depicts full-scale orchids in bloom (FIG. 39). The lithographer, Maxime Gauci, is little known. His translation of drawings by two important female botanical artists, Augusta Withers and S. A. Drake, into prints for Bateman's *Orchidaceae* ranks him among the most successful lithographers of the nineteenth century, owing to his sensitive portrayal of light and modulation of the natural forms found in the original watercolors.

39. **Tiger orchid**, hand-colored lithograph
    by Maxime Gauci, English, active 1810–1846
    after Augusta Innes Withers, English, 1793–1864
    in *The Orchidaceae of Mexico and Guatemala* (London, 1837–1843)
    by James Bateman, English, 1811–1897

The information conveyed by a color illustration may differ from an image executed in black and white. The clarity of an uncolored print was often better suited to the analysis of plant morphology, whereas color was more appealing to gardeners or amateur botanists. Some publications integrated black and white with color on the same page as a means to address both needs, as in William Roxburgh's *Plants of the Coast of Coromandel* (London, 1795–1819; FIG. 40). The artists from India that Roxburgh employed for his publication revealed an affection for brilliant color and stylized surface textures in their designs. Before advances in color printing during the late eighteenth century, coloring was sometimes left to the discretion of the owner, who might commission a colorist to enhance a publication; the original artist was seldom involved. Only copies colored under the supervision of the artist or with the original drawings at hand ensured consistency.

40. **Kradon,** hand-colored etching
after an unknown Indian artist
in *Plants of the Coast of Coromandel,* vol. 3 (London, 1819)
by William Roxburgh, Scottish, 1751–1815

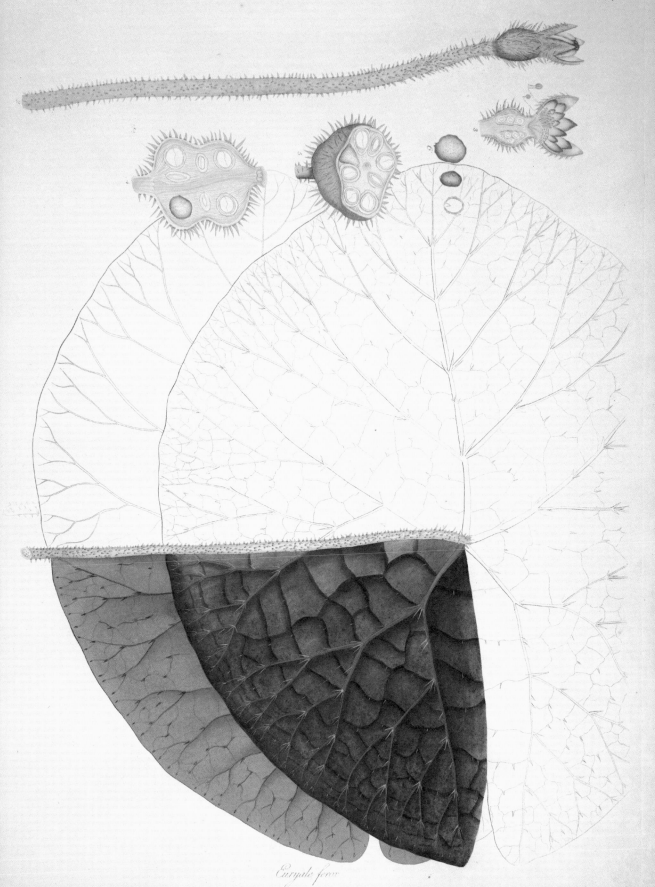

Euryale ferox

The Garden also owns an extraordinarily rare and valuable copy of Pierre Joseph Redouté's *Les Liliacées* (Paris, 1805–1816; FIG. 41). Each colored plate is bound next to an uncolored impression; close examination of the black images reveal a stipple-etching technique. Stippling entails the use of an etching needle or the roulette, a wheeled tool, to create small dots which add tone and create areas of shading within a print. The colored impressions benefited from Redouté's 1786 visit to London where he encountered a form of intaglio printing known as *à la poupée* (shaped like a doll's head), in which color was applied locally to a plate with a small rag. Careful inking and wiping made it possible to print a multicolored image with only a single run through the press, unlike traditional methods that required a new plate for every color. The process is so difficult that it is rarely used, even today.

Bromelia Ananas   *Ananas cultivé*

41. **Pineapple**, stipple etching with roulette, line engraving,
and *à-la-poupée* color printing with an adjoining black impression (left)
by de Gouy, French, active 18th century
after Pierre Joseph Redouté, French, 1759–1840
in *Les Liliacées,* vol. 8 (Paris, 1816)
by Alire Raffeneau-Delile, French, 1778–1850

A continuing fascination with new printing techniques is perhaps best represented with Alois Auer's development of nature printing in Vienna in 1853. Henry Bradbury patented the process in England and used it to illustrate Thomas Moore's *The Ferns of Great Britain and Ireland* (London, 1855; FIGS. 32, 42). Nature printing involved placing a plant between a steel plate and a lead plate. Great pressure was applied so that a near faultless impression of the plant was formed in the lead. Stronger elements, such as the central spine of the leaf, would create a deep recess, while the most delicate tendrils would leave only very fine lines in the soft lead plate. To create a sturdy facsimile, the lead plate was galvanized in copper. This ingenious method allowed for various depths of line in the copper. Several colors could be applied individually, by hand, to different areas of the plate, and then all colors would be printed together from one pull of the press. The print captures an exact impression of the plant with scientific precision, artfully arranged and colored by the printer to accentuate the natural beauty and details of each specimen. In a sense, the draftsman and printmaker are omitted from the illustration process altogether. Though potentially very useful for botanists, especially for thin and intricate plants like ferns and seaweeds, the process was extremely expensive, and very few nature-printed botanical works were published after 1860.

42. **Lady fern**, nature print
by Henry Bradbury, English, 1829–1860
in *The Ferns of Great Britain and Ireland* (London, 1855)
by Thomas Moore, English, 1821–1887

Plate XXX.

Athyrium Filix-fœmina.

Protea   *mellifera*

Plate 7.

During the first half of the nineteenth century, new chemical dyes enhanced illustrations and availed colorists of additional choices when attempting to mimic the color of a flower. Cobalt blue became available in 1802, followed by strontium yellow in 1830. Some of these bright hues turn up in Arabella Roupell's *Specimens of the Flora of South Africa by a Lady* (London, 1849, FIG. 43).

43. **Sugar bush**, hand-colored lithograph
after Arabella E. Roupell, South African, 1817–1914
in *Specimens of the Flora of South Africa
by a Lady* (London, 1849)
by Arabella E. Roupell

CONVENTIONS AND VARIATIONS

Although factors such as color and medium which influence the look of an illustration may vary, certain conventions recur throughout the centuries. The earliest botanical publications established standards for plant illustration, presenting plants as isolated specimens silhouetted on a blank background. This principle of composition governs the majority of works represented in this catalog and continues today in the Missouri Botanical Garden's own publications. Even deviations from this model tend to portray a silhouetted plant.

The tulips in Robert Thornton's *The Temple of Flora* (London, 1807) inhabit a backdrop purporting to be Holland, yet their blooms remain easily recognizable (FIG. 1). Abraham Munting's *Phytographia curiosa* (Amsterdam, 1702) presents a well-outlined drawing of the great masterwort plant in a wonderful *trompe l'oeil* image: the artist wants the viewer to believe that the masterwort has just been brought in from the field and laid down on a tattered old print showing a rural landscape with villagers, dogs, and a horseman (FIG. 44).

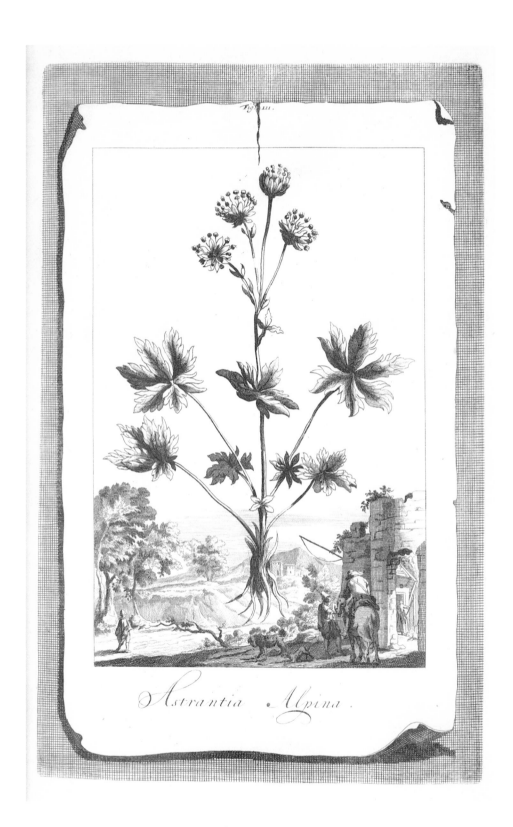

Astrantia Alpina.

44. **Great masterwort,** etching
by an unknown artist
in *Phytographia curiosa* (Amsterdam, 1702)
by Abraham Munting, Dutch, 1626–1683
and Franz Kiggelaer, Dutch, died 1722

It is clear that the favored system of classification plays a part in how a plant is depicted. Illustrators were apt to include only data considered pertinent and to exclude aspects of a plant which played no part in its classification. Many Renaissance herbals featured root systems since they were key ingredients in remedies (FIGS. 4, 10). However, after Linnaeus established a system of classification based on a plant's sexual organs, the blossom figured much more prominently and the root almost disappeared, unless it was a bulb or had some economic significance (FIGS. 26, 45, 46, 48). The root begins to reappear in botanical illustrations in the beginning of the nineteenth century when classifications considered the entire plant (FIGS. 29, 32).

45. **Brazilian star amaryllis with butterfly,** hand-colored aquatint
by Robert Havell Jr., English, 1793–1878
after Priscilla Susan Bury, English, c.1800–c.1869
in *A Selection of Hexandrian Plants* (London, 1831–1834)
by Priscilla Susan Bury

46. Raspberries, hand-colored etching by Gottlieb Friedrich Abel, German, born 1763 in *Beschreibung und Abbildung der Deutschland seltener wildwachsenden und einiger bereits naturalisierten Holz-Arten* (Stuttgart, 1803) by Johann Daniel von Reitter, German, 1759–1811

Stylistic conventions also contribute to the look of a botanical illustration. The etched stems and blooms in the bouquet depicted in Jacques Bailly's *Nova racolta di varie...fiori* (Rome, 1681) possess a brilliant Baroque dynamism, expressed primarily through composition: the stems and ribbons twist and turn, the blossoms tilt and cascade—all of which lead the eye animatedly around the arrangement (FIG. 47). The later Rococo style infused botanical illustrations with sinuous floating lines, apparent in Nikolaus Joseph Jacquin's *Plantarum rariorum* (Vienna, 1797–1804; FIG. 48). Its Rococo-influenced illustrations appear almost weightless when compared to floral depictions from the Renaissance and Baroque eras. Yet within the same period, or even the same publication, the quality of illustration may vary, a phenomenon due not only to different hands at work, but the type of model used by draftsmen. Models ranged from live plants and dried specimens to pages from manuscripts and other pictorial records.

Illustrations are products of their time, making each a wonderful resource in our understanding of plant history and illustration. Although today photography has become the dominant medium in scientific publications, it has not completely replaced botanical drawing. The draftsman can clearly demarcate intricate plant structures like the veins of a leaf or the ovaries of a flower better than the photographer. With pen and pencil, the draftsman can focus, analyze, and dissect a plant and add shading and volume to isolate and emphasize particular elements. A draftsman can also combine all the disparate parts of a plant into one intelligible design.

Sperone di Cavaliere turchino

Anemone semplice color di Carne, con li semi pauonazzi

Anemone doppio con frondi bianche, e frondine di mezzo di color di Carne

Iacinto Bianco

Anemone con frondi bianche, e rosse, con frondine di mezzo rosine

47. **Bouquet of anemones, hyacinth, and delphinium,** etching with engraved letters
by Arnold van Westerhout, Flemish, 1651–1725
after Jacques Bailly, French, c.1634–1679
in *Nova racolta di varie...fiori* (Rome, 1681)
by Jacques Bailly

Since the fifteenth century, botanical illustrations have played a significant role in plant research and have represented the close collaboration between artists and botanists. These books stand as products of lively centers of research, and this vital tradition continues at the Missouri Botanical Garden. Today, as species are becoming extinct at an unprecedented rate, the Missouri Botanical Garden's research division strives to discover new information about plants, promote the efforts of the botanical research community, and disseminate information to a wide audience. Aided by illustrators, its scientists carry out the most active and geographically widespread botanical research program in the world. ❧

48. **African corn lily**; hand-colored etching
by Johann Scharf, Austrian, 1765–1794
or Martin Sedelmayer, Austrian, 1776–1799
or Franz Anton von Scheidel, Austrian, 1731–1801
in *Plantarum rariorum horti caesarei
Schoenbrunnensis*, vol. 1 (Vienna, 1797)
by Nicolaus Joseph Jacquin, Dutch (active Austria), 1712–1817

T.24.

Ixia miniata.

List of Figures

Aldini, Tobia and Pietro Castelli. *Exactissima descriptio rariorum quarundam plantarum*. Rome, 1625.

Bailly, Jacques. *Nova racolta di varie...fiori*. Rome, 1681.

Bateman, James. *The Orchidaceae of Mexico and Guatemala*. London, 1837–1843.

Benalio, Bernardino and Giovanni Tacuino, eds. *Hortus sanitatis*. Venice, 1511.

Blume, Karl Ludwig. *Rumphia, sive, Commentationes botanicæ imprimis de plantis Indiæ Orientalis*. vol. 2. Leiden, 1835.

Brunfels, Otto. *Herbarum vivae eicones*. Strasbourg, 1530.

Bury, Priscilla Susan. *A Selection of Hexandrian Plants*. London, 1831–1834.

Catesby, Mark. *The Natural History of Carolina, Florida, and the Bahama Islands*. London, 1754.

Colonna, Fabio. *Phytobasanos*. Naples, 1592.

Commelin, Caspar. *Horti medici amstelædamensis plantae rariores*. Leiden, 1706.

Duhamel du Monceau, Henri Louis. *Traité des arbres fruitiers*. vol. 2. Paris, 1768.

Duret, Claude. *Histoire admirable des plantes et herbes esmerueillables et miraculeuses en nature*. Paris, 1605.

Ferrari, Giovanni Battista. *Flora overo cultura di fiori*. Rome, 1638.

———. *Hesperides*. Rome, 1646.

Fuchs, Leonhart. *De historia stirpium*. Basel, 1542.

Gart der Gesundheyt. Published by Peter Schöffer. Mainz, 1485.

Gerard, John. *The Herball*. Revised by Thomas Johnson. London, 1636.

Grandville, Jean Jacques and Taxile Delord. *Les Fleurs animées*. Paris, 1846–1847.

Grew, Nehemiah. *The Anatomy of Plants*. London, 1682.

Hooke, Robert. *Micrographia*. London, 1665.

Hooker, Sir Joseph Dalton. *Illustrations of Himalayan Plants*. London, 1855.

Hornemann, Jens Wilken, ed. *Flora Danica*. vol. 12, issue 34. Copenhagen, 1830.

———. *Flora Danica*. vol. 13, issue 37. Copenhagen, 1836.

Jacquin, Nicolaus Joseph. *Plantarum rariorum horti caesarei Schoenbrunnensis*. vol. 1. Vienna, 1797.

Lambert, Aylmer Bourke. *A Description of the Genus Pinus*. vol. 1. London, 1803.

Laroche, François de. *Les Liliacées*. vol. 7. Published by Pierre Joseph Redouté. Paris, 1813.

Lindley, John. *Pomologia Britannica*. vol. 3. London, 1841.

Linnaeus, Carl. *Hortus Cliffortianus*. Amsterdam, 1738.

Martius, Karl Friedrich Philipp von. *Historia naturalis palmarum*. vols. 1 and 2. parts 6, 7, 9. Leipzig, 1837–1849.

Mattioli, Pietro Andrea. *Commentarii*. Venice, 1583.

———. Woodblock of peas for *Commentarii*. Prague, 1562.

Miscellanea curiosa medico–physica. vol. 2. Published by Academia Naturæ Curiosorum. Leipzig, 1671.

Moore, Thomas. *The Ferns of Great Britain and Ireland*. London, 1855.

Munting, Abraham and Franz Kiggelaer. *Phytographia curiosa*. Amsterdam and Leiden, 1702.

Raffeneau–Delile, Alire. *Flore d'Égypte* from *Description de l'Égypte*. vol. 2. Paris, 1813.

———. *Les Liliacées*. vol. 8. Published by Pierre Joseph Redouté. Paris, 1816.

Redouté, Pierre Joseph. see Laroche and Raffeneau–Delile.

Reitter, Johann Daniel von. *Beschreibung und Abbildung der Deutschland seltener wildwachsenden und einiger bereits naturalisierten Holz–Arten*. Stuttgart, 1803.

Reneaulme, Paul de. *Specimen historiae plantarum*. Paris, 1611.

Roupell, Arabella E. *Specimens of the Flora of South Africa by a Lady*. London, 1849.

Roxburgh, William. *Plants of the Coast of Coromandel*. vol. 3. London, 1819.

Seba, Albert. *Locupletissimi rerum naturalium thesauri*. Amsterdam, 1734–1765.

Sloane, Sir Hans. *A Voyage to the Islands Madera, Barbadoes, Nieves, S. Christophers and Jamaica*. London, 1707–1725.

Sweerts, Emanuel. *Florilegium*. Amsterdam, 1647–1654.

Thornton, Robert John. *The Philosophy of Botany*. vol. 3. London, 1810.

———. *The Temple of Flora* from *A New Illustration of the Sexual System of Linnaeus*. London, 1807.

Trew, Cristoph Jacob. *Plantae selectae*. parts 1 and 2. Nuremburg, 1750–1751.

Volkamer, Johann Christoph. *Hesperides norimbergenses*. Nuremberg, 1713.

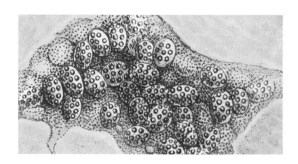

Above:
detail of **Papaya**
see Fig. 26

Editor: Elizabeth McNulty
Designer: Justin Visnesky
Imaging: Fred Keusenkothen

Printed in St. Louis by The Printing Source

This book was typeset in Sabon:
A descendant of the types of Claude Garamond, Sabon was designed by
Jan Tschichold in 1964 and jointly released by Stempel, Linotype, and
Monotype foundries. The Roman design is based on a Garamond specimen
printed by Konrad F. Berner, who was married to the widow of another
printer, Jacques Sabon. The italic design is based on types by Robert
Granjon, a contemporary of Garamond's.

The paper used in this publication meets the minimum requirements of the
American National Standard for Information Sciences—Permanence of Paper
for Printed Library Materials, ANSI Z39.48–1984.

All the works illustrated in this catalog belong to the Missouri Botanical Garden.
For exhibition at the Saint Louis Art Museum, one hundred works were chosen
from forty-four publications; the process of rebinding and repairing these books
allowed for the display of some individual sheets. Citation standards may vary
between the Art Museum and the Garden. For this catalog, citations refer to the
common name of the plant rather than the Latin binomial. Often we cite
illustrations from different volumes of a single multivolume publication that was
published over a span of many years. Although the volumes may share the same
title, they infrequently share the same authors, artists, or the same year of
publication. Captions refer only to those persons involved in the making of that
particular volume and image, and we give only that volume's publication date.
When citing the illustration, we first distinguish the printmaker, then the
draftsman (e.g., Arnold van Westerhout after Jacques Bailly). The draftsmen are
always identified with the term "after" preceding their name. Sometimes the
artists involved in a publication are unknown today. In such instances, we list
the names of the authors or publishers as reference.

The Missouri Botanical Garden has established itself as a leader in the field of
digitization, working to bring rare books and materials to the web since 1995.
With a state-of-the-art digitization lab staffed by trained photographers, the
Garden has helped set the standards for rare book digitization projects
worldwide. Through the generous support of the Andrew W. Mellon
Foundation, dozens of beautifully illustrated books can be viewed in their
entirety at www.illustratedgarden.org.